THE
SECRET HISTORY OF
FAIRIES

J. RENISON

Kandour Ltd

Published by

Kandour Limited,

Monticello House,

45 Russell Square,

London,

WC1B 4JP

United Kingdom

This edition printed in 2007

First published 2007

10 9 8 7 6 5 4 3 2 1

Author: Jessica Renison

Editor: John Taylor

Design and Layout: Domex e-Data Pvt Limited

Proof reader: Tobias Grimshaw

Production: Karen Lomax & Carol Titchener

Design concepts: Alex Ingr

Text and Design Copyright © Kandour Limited 2007

Printed and bound in Singapore

ISBN 13: 978-0-681-16367-6

Contents

Fairies have been around for longer than you or I could ever imagine. Of all supernatural beings, they are the ones most intimately involved in our daily lives, and they are as old as nature itself. And yet we hardly ever see them. Have you ever wondered why? Well, one reason is that they are so well hidden in the ordinary things around us, like trees, stones, streams, haystacks and flowers that we take them entirely for granted. But there are other reasons, some of them sinister, why fairies hardly ever visit the world of humans anymore. In this book, we will attempt to piece together some fragments from the secret history of fairies so that we can learn to appreciate more fully their hidden world all around us.

What Fairies Look Like

Fairies are miniature beings, small enough to fit through keyholes and certainly not large enough to carry a potato on their backs – this should give you some idea of their size. They have wings which are something like the wings of a dragonfly – shimmering, multi-colored, and always changing in different lights. With their luminescent wings, they dart about so quickly that it is quite difficult to see them, especially as they can easily blend into their surroundings. Fairies have the faces of human beings, only some of their features are exaggerated, so they might have pointed ears for example, or extremely red cheeks, or tiny noses. These details, which set them apart from humans, also tend to make them look as if they are up to no good. But one thing that you can say about fairies' faces is that they are always remarkably pretty.

Character and Temperament

In character and temperament, fairies are – it has to be said – generally mischievous. There is no denying that they enjoy playing tricks and having fun. Usually, this is quite innocent and harmless, but on occasion it can get out of hand and lead to them stealing items from the world of humans. If you asked them, you would probably find that they fully intended to return these items, they just hadn't quite got around to it yet. Although naughty themselves, fairies deplore bad behavior in others. They are particularly averse to bad manners and bad tempers; the fairy code of behavior demands cheerfulness at all times.

The other aspect of their character that stands out is their love of order: they are extremely neat, so a fairy in your house can actually be a blessing (as well as being somewhat troublesome when they are in a mischievous mood). If you find that you frequently lose things, you can be sure there is a fairy somewhere about who has been tidying up after you and putting things where you can't find them.

Fairies are immeasurably fond of music and dance, but they don't just party all the time, they can also work hard when required. Their delicate hands are very precise and can carry out intricate work with ease: thus the fairies have become a race of capable craftspeople and can fashion small objects like shoes, chairs or bows and arrows out of little more than what nature provides.

Fairy Handicrafts

Here are some common fairy handicrafts. See if you can guess what they are made out of. Some of the answers have been given.

Soup bowl	Acorn cup
Bow and arrow	?
Dish-cloth	Woven from a spider's web
Shoes	Nut shells
Hat	?
Fork	?
Chair	?

Fairies are also adept at spinning and weaving, grinding wheat and corn for bread and metalwork of all sorts.

Fairy Food

Fairies live mainly off food that has been discarded by humans. There is plenty of this to go around and they would never go hungry if they lived entirely on the remnants of human food, but they do also have their own food for interest, variety and freshness. Food that is specifically fairy food includes silver weed, a root turned up by the plowing machines in spring, heather stalks, and the milk of the red deer. Fairies tend to eat little and often, munching on crumbs, roots and seeds as and when they find them, rather than sitting down for a big meal. On Feast Days and for family celebrations however, they would all sit together and share what everyone had managed to gather that day. You would be quite amazed to see how much a fairy can consume on a Feast Day, given their diminutive size.

Fairy Clothing

Fairies make their clothing out of what nature provides and they are surprisingly inventive with a relatively limited range of materials. They generally wear green, brown and red, as these are the colors most commonly available: some of the most traditional materials are moss, leaves and berries. In some accounts of fairy sightings, it has been reported that they wear pointed hats. These are most likely to be made from the husks of nuts or from certain flower heads. Fairies are not, on the whole, vain about their appearance, but they do take care to look neat and well turned-out.

Fairy Paraphernalia

Fairies are often pictured with twinkling wands, but this is somewhat misleading, because it is certainly not the case that every fairy would possess this coveted accessory. Fairies have to earn their wands by proving their maturity and a sober sense of responsibility. As you can imagine, very few fairies manage to prove this and so, very few earn their wands. Their wands are like their furniture and clothing, made out of nature's own materials, and can vary from a willow twig to an icicle, from a dragonfly's leg to a blade of grass. The magic lies not in the material itself, but in the enchantment that is laid over it, by the words chanted at its christening. Once it has been brought into being, a fairy wand is a very powerful tool and

it could cause great harm — on the level of bringing about avalanches or droughts – if it got into the wrong hands. This is the reason for the care that is taken over the distribution of wands. Though the wands themselves are in fact highly sensitive to the hand that holds them and are able to melt away if they detect the wrong hand, they are not infallible and have been known to be fooled by a clever impostor wishing to bring destruction on mankind. Fairy wands are only really used for quite minor spell-working like fixing what is broken, finding what is lost, and forging friendships between enemies. However, there is a slight contradiction here, as the things being broken or lost in the first place were probably the work of other, less mature fairies, so fairy wands are often used for undoing what other fairies have done wrong.

The other essential accessory, if you were to believe the pictures in children's books, is fairy dust. This is sometimes shown shooting off the end of a wand or bursting out behind a flying fairy, in a cloud of sparkles. It looks terribly glamorous, but fairy dust actually has a very ordinary, even humdrum, purpose. It is used either to cast invisibility or to warn other flying creatures of their presence, as headlights do to other cars on the road. So, although wands and fairy dust are what makes us envy fairies most of all, there are in reality, very few who possess either of these, and they would not be the sort to show them off unnecessarily. The fairy, Tinker Bell in Peter Pan uses her fairy dust to make humans fly, but unfortunately, this hardly ever happens. Tinker Bell had special powers given to her because it was her job to make children believe in fairies.

Fairies Hidden in Nature

Fairies can live anywhere, but they are most at home, around woodland and water. They love shiny stones like marble and jade, so they are often on the lookout for these. One of their favorite pastimes is polishing stones with their skirts, until they shine so brightly that they can see their laughing faces reflected in them. Fairies also enjoy playing in clear running streams, jumping from stone to stone, and daring each other to jump onto the back of leaping fish. In fact, the sound that is often mistaken for the babbling water rushing over stones, is actually fairy laughter, cleverly disguised.

Another favorite fairy haunt is a strawberry field. They love climbing through the tangle of branches in the sweet smell of the juicy, red berries, and they can never resist a straw fight. Many a farmer, has been baffled in the morning, by the terrible mess of his straw, which was fine when he left it but now seems to be all over the place. It comes as no surprise, that by far the most frequent instances of fairy sightings have been reported by farmers. Farmers are known to rise early and get to their fields before dawn on some occasions, so it is inevitable that sometimes they will catch fairies still in the midst of their night-time revels.

The Secret History Of Fairies

The other natural home of fairies is in the common back garden. Here, they are particularly drawn to fragrant beds of herbs, which they literally use as beds. People have been known to build fairy homes in their gardens, similar to birds' nests, and to hang wind chimes so that the fairies can dance to their beautiful music. You can read some more about fairies and gardens a little later.

The fairies' favorite trees are Oak, Ash and Thorn, and they protect these fiercely; so you should always beware of harming one of these trees. Fairies who live in trees enjoy playing with squirrels, who are quite similar to them in temperament – both like to scamper and snatch.

As you probably know, fairies often live in flowers but they take on the color of the flower they live in, so it is very difficult to see them.

Fairies and Flowers

As well as disguising themselves to look like the flowers they inhabit, fairies lend their own particular qualities to their chosen flowers and become a part of them. Here is a run-down of some of the flowers favored by fairies, so that you will know what to expect from these flowers:

Angelica

Inhabited by spirited fairies, angelica brings good fortune and vitality. A good pick-me-up.

Buttercup

Fairies of the buttercup are compassionate and tender towards humans. The golden glow that buttercups leave on the human skin, is a sign of the warmth these fairies feel towards us.

Bluebell

If ever a bluebell rings in your garden, it is a warning to beware that a malignant fairy will be somewhere nearby.

Carnation

The fairies who frequent carnations are the ones who have the power to heal animals.

Cowslip

One of the most precious of all fairy flowers, the cowslip has the power to uncover hidden fairy treasure.

Dandelion

This is a more everyday, practical flower as far as fairies are concerned, because they use it to make drinks.

Foxglove

Although its name is somewhat misleading, this flower actually makes an ideal hat or pair of gloves for a fairy, not a fox!

Iris

Iris was the Greek goddess of the rainbow, so naturally fairies who frequent this flower are multi-colored and changeable.

The Secret History Of Fairies

Lavender

The fairies who live in this flower are by nature protective and have healing powers

Lilac

This flower that attracts fairies are musically inclined – no one knows quite why.

Marigold

The fairies who hold this flower dear are versed in the mysterious workings of thunderstorms.

Pansy

Sometimes used by fairies as a love potion.

Primrose

This flower is believed to give fairies their power of invisibility.

Ragwort

This is more of a grass than a flower, but its interesting

part in the fairy's life is that, it acts as a kind of horse, for them to ride.

Tulip

Fairies associated with this flower have knowledge of the significance of events. They can see behind the surface as to what is really going on.

Violet

This flower is blessed, as it is sacred to the fairy queen.

How to See Fairies

One of the most frustrating things about fairies is that we rarely see the fairies themselves, but we often see evidence that they have been around. So, if you are one of those who is on a constant quest to find a fairy, you could try looking out for some of the following signs and you will at least know that fairies are somewhere nearby:

• When you see a patch of grass that has been flattened, but you can't see any reason why, you can be sure that fairies have been dancing there, the previous night.

• The next time it is frosty and there are frost patterns on your window panes, take a closer look. You might if you are lucky, see fairy footprints left behind, because frost patterns are of course the beautiful artwork of fairies.

However, if you are not content with seeing signs, and are determined to see the fairy itself, read on to discover certain secrets which can help you in your quest. There are certain times of the year that are considered particularly propitious for seeing fairies. Midsummer's Eve, on the 21st June is one of these. On this evening and this evening alone, fairies are able to use human speech, so if you listen carefully in the right places, you might discover them. In Italy, it is thought to be Twelfth Night, 6th January, that is sacred to fairies. On this night, they come into homes and leave sweets for children. During Victorian times, around May Day, women would bake sweet cakes and leave them out in the garden near a patch of thyme, as thyme was thought to be a favorite herb of the fairies. So you have to pick the right time and the

right place, but all being well, there is no reason why we shouldn't see fairies. Here are a few hints to help you along the way:

• The next time that you are walking in a field of clover, look carefully for a clover with four leaves. Pick it and lie down quietly in the grass and before long, fairies will be dancing all around you.

• Whenever you are walking by water where there are stones on the shoreline, look carefully for a stone that has had a hole bored through it by the running water. Such a stone is distinctive, because the hole has smooth edges and is perfectly round. Look through the hole and you will be looking straight into the world of fairies.

• Mushrooms are commonly used by fairies to mark the boundaries of their dancing circle, so next time you see a mushroom circle, look closely at what is inside. You may need to be quite patient, and certainly you will need very acute eyesight.

• Whenever you hear the leaves rustling in the trees, listen more closely, and if you are fortunate to have an ear that is tuned to the fairy world, as some humans do, you will hear that what you thought was the wind in the trees, is actually the fairies talking and laughing.

There are other ways to see fairies, many of which involve strengthening and improving your eyesight. Here is a recipe designed to make the eyesight more sensitive to the fairy world. It dates back to the 17th century:

"Mix, one pint of salad oil with rose and marigold water prepared from flowers picked early in the morning. Add to the mix, buds of hollyhock, thyme, hazel and marigolds plucked from an area where you believe Fairies dwell, as well as a sprig of grass from that same area. Do not use greens from your flower garden, and if you find a four - leaf clover, much better. The mixture should sit in the sun for three days. Strain the oil and apply to the eyelids to enhance your sight, but make sure it doesn't get into your eyes."

There are other ways to see fairies, many of which involve strengthening and improving your eyesight. Here is a recipe designed to make the eyesight more sensitive to the fairy world.

The Secret History Of Fairies

Fairy Disguises

Fairies often take on disguises when they wish to enter the human world. One common appearance is as an old man or old woman who offer helpful advice. They have also been known to take on the bodies of cats, so if your cat begins to behave in a peculiar manner, you never know – it may be a fairy in disguise.

Fairy Rings

Fairy rings are sometimes visible and sometimes not. The visible kind is the ring of mushrooms – usually poisonous, which is said to have grown out of the imprint of fairy feet. This, obviously, we can see, but we would be unwise to step inside it. You would not know if the other kind was there or not until you had actually stepped inside it and then of course, it would be too late. Humans can be lured inside fairy

rings, and once there, they are under the fairy's spell. Time is very different inside the fairy ring, so what might seem like minutes might actually be days. It is difficult to say what happens to humans inside these rings because few can remember precisely once they have been released from the spell. It takes a chain of humans, all holding hands and the last in the chain holding onto a tree, to pull a person who has been trapped in a fairy ring out. Humans who are taken into the fairy world have tried in the past to bring tokens back from that world as proof of where they have been, but these objects always turn into something else when they are back in the real world. A coin given by a fairy, for example, suddenly becomes an ordinary stone, once they have been released from the fairy world.

So, as you can see, fairies are an inextricable part of nature: you cannot take fairies away from nature and you cannot take nature away from the fairies. The main challenge in discovering fairies is to learn to look closely enough, so that we can see them hidden in nature all around us.

But where did they come from? How did they get here? And most importantly – what are they?

There is a vast history of belief and non-belief surrounding fairies, and many different theories around the world as to what they are. We can only really touch on these issues in this secret history, because we are more properly concerned with learning to see them and observing their behavior.

These gods and goddesses were really aspects of nature. In fact, Mother Nature herself was seen as a goddess and she had to be worshipped to ensure a prosperous and healthy land. According to the old system of belief, which is called paganism, there was a 'fairy queen', a mother-figure who presided over nature and caused the growth of flowers and fruits. She has been given many names by many different

Fairies in Pre-Christian Times

In primitive times, a person's soul was thought of as a miniature version of themselves, and it was thought that this mini person, the soul, left the body through the mouth during sleep and spent the night roaming about. The soul had to return to the body before morning when the person woke up, but until then it could take any form it wished. This idea of our soul as a miniature version of ourselves could perhaps form the basis of the origin fairies. But this is only one version of events.

Before Christianity reached the shores of Europe, the people worshipped gods and goddesses.

cultures, including Demeter, Ceres, Diana, Venus and Titania, and is also, sometimes referred to as Dame Abundance or Lady Bounty. It was said that these fairies – also called 'fays' – knew the power of words, stones and herbs. They were positive, helpful spirits who were wise in the ways of nature and knew how to harness nature's power in order to heal and promote growth.

Once the people were converted to the new religion of Christianity, they began to lose faith in

their old religion. The leaders of the Christian church taught people that worshipping the likes of goddesses or fairies was evil because it put them in place of the 'one' God. In order to stop people believing in fairies, they were demonized, or made to seem worse than they were. So, those little misdemeanors like stealing shoes left outside the door, or lapping up milk from the jug left on the window sill were turned into far more serious crimes. Suddenly, fairies got blamed for stealing babies and swapping them with 'changelings'. The 'changelings' could be a baby carved out of a piece of wood, or a sick or deformed fairy child. It was said, that the only way you could prevent your baby from being stolen from its cradle,

was to hang its father's trousers over the side of the crib, or more strangely, to hang a pair of open scissors above its cradle, which sounds a little risky! Parents who were left with a changeling would often return it to the fairies by leaving it in the woods, but some would treat the changeling with kindness, in the hope that their own child would be treated with kindness.

Once the people were converted to the new religion of Christianity, they began to lose faith in their old religion. The leaders of the Christian church taught people that worshiping the likes of goddesses or fairies was evil because it put them in place of the 'one' God.

When fairies came to be seen as harmful rather than helpful, humans began to invent various ways of keeping them at bay. It was thought that iron was a metal which repelled them, so anti-fairy charms would be made out of iron and hung in the doorway of the house. It was also thought that the sign of the cross, a sign associated with Christianity and therefore seen as the opposite of what the fairies represented, would frighten them off, as they would not be able to look at it directly. In fact, this was the idea behind the open scissors, which formed an iron cross above the baby's cradle.

The Secret History Of Fairies

Some cultures say that fairies are spirits – the souls of the dead who are fit neither for heaven nor for hell, and so have to hover restlessly in between. One definition refers to them as 'a host of supernatural beings and spirits who occupy a limbo between heaven and hell'. Others say, that fairies are real human beings, the ancestors of pagan people who went into hiding long ago, out of fear of the brutal Christians who threatened their lives for believing in the wrong God. Still others say that they are angels who were thrown out of heaven for rebelling against God. There is a story that the fallen angels, who tried to overthrow the Almighty, landed on earth, but are not meant to be here and so they wander about, still immortal and unable to die, but with no real home where they belong.

The Scandinavian view of fairies is different from that found anywhere else. According to their legends about the origins of fairies, after Adam and Eve were expelled from the Garden of Eden, they went on to have large numbers of children. There were so many that they became quite unruly and bedraggled, so much so that Eve was ashamed of them, and when God called on her to present her children to him, she hid some of the worst and showed him only the best. God, naturally, knew what she was doing and he proclaimed: "Let those who were hidden from me become the hidden people," which is a name that some still apply to the fairies.

Fairy Names

In our search to discover just exactly what a fairy is, it is interesting to look at the history of the word 'fairy' itself. In old times, the word for bewitched or enchanted was 'fey', a word which originated from the word 'fate'. To be in 'feyerie' was to be in a state of enchantment, and this eventually became the word 'fairy', and was applied both to those who were enchanted and to those who caused enchantment.

However, fairies are not just called 'fairies'. They have been given many other names by many different people, often in an attempt to keep them happy and ward off ill-luck.

Fair Folk is what the Welsh sometimes call them.

Good Neighbors is from Scotland. The idea behind this is that the fairies might be listening and if they heard themselves spoken of as 'good neighbors', they might act like good neighbors. They hoped to prevent the fairies from stealing and playing nasty tricks by speaking well of them. For the same reason, the Irish refer to them as Honest Folk or Good People.

The Green Children is a name which appears in medieval literature and it refers to the way fairies often disguise themselves in green, to make themselves invisible in their woodland home.

The Secret History Of Fairies

The Silent People is another name that has been used by Irish and Scottish people in the past. The Celtic word for silent is 'suth' and the fairies are known as the silent ones because they move noiselessly, coming and going and often taking things without anyone realizing they have even been there.

An important point to remember is that fairies do not like their real names to be spoken aloud. This is why over the years we have developed various ways of referring to them without using their real names.

Fairy Classification

So, as we have established, fairies are not all of one sort. Though they all belong to the fairy race and are almost all (though not all) Celtic in origin, that is Scottish, Irish or Welsh – they are fiercely nationalistic and don't like being muddled up with each other. In this brief history of fairies, we can only sketch an outline of the different fairy races and hope they will not be offended if we mistakenly mix them up with each other.

Scottish Fairies

Scottish fairies can be divided into the 'Seelie' variety and the 'Unseelie' variety. The Seelie are the blessed fairies, who only carry out beneficial acts and are friendly towards humans. They are heroic in their deeds, travel in groups and in Scottish folklore, are depicted as a stream of light riding on the night air.

The Unseelie are, as you might have guessed, malicious and only carry out, malevolent acts. They are ugly and take pleasure in bringing harm to humans. They too travel on the night air, but they make themselves invisible so as to be more frightening and they howl and cackle as they fly. The Unseelie fairies are thought to be the souls of the dead who cannot rest: filled with envy for the human race, they often abduct humans to make them their slaves.

There is a document from the 19th century, which supposedly records the departure of the fairies

from Scotland, but it is unlikely that if indeed they left at all, they left for good. The scene of their departure was the Burn of Eathie.

On a Sabbath morning... the inmates of this little hamlet had all gone to church, all except a herd-boy, and a little girl, his sister, who were lounging beside one of the cottages; when, just as the shadow of the garden-dial had fallen on the line of noon, they saw a long cavalcade ascending out of the ravine through the wooded hollow. It winded among the knolls and bushes; and, turning round the northern gable of the cottage beside which the sole spectators of the scene were stationed, began to ascend the eminence toward the south. The horses were shaggy,

diminutive things, speckled dun and grey; the riders, stunted, misgrown, ugly creatures, attired in antique jerkins of plaid, long grey cloaks, and little red caps, from under which their wild uncombed locks shot out over their cheeks and foreheads. The boy and his sister stood gazing in utter dismay and astonishment, as rider after rider, each one more uncouth and dwarfish than the one that had preceded it, passed the cottage, and disappeared among the brushwood which at that period covered the hill, until at length the entire rout, except the last rider, who lingered a few yards behind the others, had gone by.

'What are ye, little mannie? and where are ye going?' inquired the boy, his curiosity getting the better of his fears and his prudence. 'Not of the race of Adam,' said the creature, turning for a moment in his saddle: 'the People of Peace shall never more be seen in Scotland.'

- The Old Red Sandstone by Hugh Miller

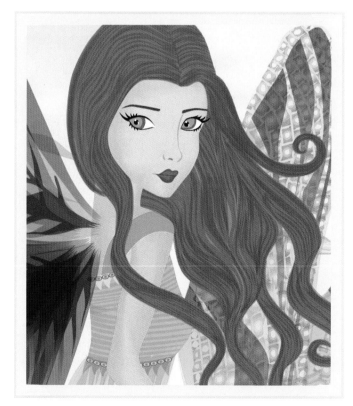

Ireland

In Ireland, one of the few places left where fairies are still allowed a home – fairies are thought to be descendants of the goddess Dana and it is said that back in the Bronze Age, they were the first to discover silver and gold. These followers of the goddess Dana, called in the Irish language 'Tuatha De Danaan', built great stone temples to worship the sun and the moon. These very same fairies are still thought to live on in the ancient burial mounds, that are scattered throughout the Irish countryside. Because, they live underground, they are rarely seen, and since they never see the light of day, their growth has been stunted over the years. This explains their small size and is another reason why it is difficult to see them even when they do venture out.

Irish fairies have a king, rather than a queen. His name is Finvarra, and like all the rest of his clan, he is a skilled warrior. He has a beautiful wife called Donagh, but he is not content with this and is known to steal brides-to-be, just before they get married. Fairies of this clan are excellent riders and are famous for their horses, which can carry them faster than lightening over land or sea.

There is another group of fairies in Ireland who live in a lake called the Lough Lean. Their ruler is O'Donoghue and every May Day, he rides out of the lake on his horse.

Wales

Wales is home to a whole host of fairy clans. They are known as the Tylwyth Teg – the Fair Family – which suggests how close they are to their human neighbors. These fairies are seen as mortal men and women, but they are part of a different race. In the 16th century, there were stories of a race of people called the Red Fairies living in the Great Dark Wood. They lived underground and had bright red hair and they stole cattle by night. When we look at them now, we can see that they were most probably a band of outlaws living in the woods, but at that time, they were thought to have supernatural powers, and there is a legend based around their dark powers which survives into the

modern day. According to this legend, a knight called Baron Owen decided to attack the Red Fairies at the head of an army of warriors. He hung a hundred of their men, but spared the women and children. One woman begged him to spare the life of her grown son, but he refused, so she cursed him, vowing: "This breast has nursed other sons than he, who will yet wash their hands in thy blood, Baron Owen!" Soon after, Baron Owen was attacked at night by a band of men who killed him and washed their hands in his blood.

There is a legend in Wales that long, long ago, every New Year's Day, a door would appear in the side of a great rock next to a certain lake. All those who dared to enter found, that it lead to a passage, that ended on the island in the middle of the lake. This island had a beautiful garden kept by the Gwrgedd Annwn, who would serve wonderful food to the travelers and treat them as honored guests.

They warned the fortunate mortals that the doorway was a secret and that nothing could be taken from the garden. One mortal took a single flower from the garden and as soon as he touched the soil of earth, all of the other travelers were expelled and the doorway was closed, never to reopen again.

The Scottish, Irish and Welsh are the broad groups of fairies, but there are also, within these nationalities, different types of fairies. They can be divided into, the solitary and the trooping. Solitary fairies, like the banshee for example, live and work alone. They are not part of any group and do not need to be. They are seen as a sort of 'aristocracy' of the fairy world. The other sort is the trooping fairies, who belong to a band of fellow fairies and travel around in groups. Trooping fairies would not operate alone: they only exist as part of a crowd, and they are seen as the 'peasantry' of the fairy world.

Asrai

These creatures are delicate, female fairies. They live underground and come out only at night because they are so delicate, that sunlight would melt them.

Banshee

This is a female spirit attached to a family. When a member of the family is about to die, the banshee 'wails' with grief.

Brownies

These are helpful and friendly fairies who attach themselves to a particular family and remain loyal to them.

Elves

Elves, like dwarves and gnomes, are creatures of the earth. They travel in groups and are hardworking.

Gnomes

Gnomes live underground and are particularly skilled at metalwork. They make swords and shields out of metals that they mine from the hills.

Goblins

These are ugly and malicious creatures. They work ill on the human race, but are not very intelligent, so they are usually controlled in groups by a Mage.

Dryads

The Dryads are the tree-dwelling spirits. They were worshipped by Druids in old times.

Dwarves

Not at all like our image of delicate fairies, dwarves are short and thick-set, but very powerful. They age very quickly and by seven years of age, already have grey beards. Generally, they cannot endure sunlight which quickly turns them to stone, but they can overcome this with spells and potions.

Gwyllion

These are Scottish water-fairies, malevolent in their natures. They lurk by remote mountain paths and intentionally mislead travelers. They do this quite surreptitiously by sitting on a rock beside the path, silently watching passers-by, making them feel so uncomfortable and so nervous, that they end up losing their way.

Leprechauns

These tiny creatures are found in Ireland. They are mischievous and enjoy playing cruel jokes on humans, but they can disappear in an instant, so they are impossible to catch. They are particularly active on St. Patrick's Day.

Mermaids

Mermaids are water spirits who are human from the waist up, but have the tail of a fish. They have beautiful, seductive voices, and their songs have been known to lure fishermen to their deaths.

Pixies

These are mischievous fairies who enjoy playing tricks on humans, but not in a nasty way. They often disguise themselves as hedgehogs and have been known to steal horses to ride (not whilst disguised as hedgehogs, because that would look very odd indeed!)

Shefro

Shefro are male fairies who can be recognized by their distinctive garb——green coats and red hats.

Sidhee

Pronounced 'shee', this is the name for Irish fairies who live underground in burial mounds.

Spriggans

Spriggans appear in stories as grotesque creatures who are naturally small, but can inflate themselves to a gigantic size. These are the sort of destructive and dangerous spirits who steal human children and leave repulsively, ugly baby Spriggans in their place.

Spriggans appear in stories as grotesque creatures who are naturally small, but can inflate themselves to a gigantic size. These are the sort of destructive and dangerous spirits who steal human children and leave repulsively ugly baby Spriggans in their place.

Fairies in Victorian Times

After years of not being believed in, fairies made something of a comeback during Victorian times. This was really their heyday: they were believed in and treasured, they had their portraits drawn and painted, they had jewelry made in their honor, had poems and books written about them. The Victorians believed that fairies lived at the bottom of the garden, in the wild part where it is all overgrown and tangled. They used to put stone statues of fairies in their gardens as a way of showing the fairies that they were liked and admired.

Trolls

Trolls, who in stories traditionally live under bridges terrorizing travelers, are terrified of daylight.

Water Fairies

Unpredictable! as they can be friends or foe.

It can be somewhat startling to learn of this whole host of fairy beings, some of whom are nothing like our enchanting image of delicate, cheerful spirits, but do not be too alarmed – the fairies you read about in this book are mostly of the delicate kind. The others – the ugly and the evil spirits – may have crept into the fairy realm, and it certainly pays to know about them, but they do not in our opinion count as true fairies.

It was around this time that the artist Cicely Mary Barker invented the Flower Fairies. Her first book appeared in 1923, and it featured fairies dressed up to represent different flowers. Cicely hand-made the flower costumes, before she painted the fairies dressed in them, and because she didn't have much money, she unpicked each costume after she had finished, so that she could re-use the fabric.

A Fairy Hoax

There is a wonderful, true story about some girls who believed so strongly in fairies that they managed to convince thousands of other people of their existence too. It is known as, 'The case of the Cottingley fairies' and it is one of the most intriguing episodes, in the whole secret history of fairies.

The Secret History Of Fairies

These true events – which will be told in full so that the reader can judge for him or herself – took place just before the end of the First World War In 1918. An 11 year-old girl called Frances Griffiths, who lived in England, wrote to her friend back in South Africa where she herself used to live. The letter went like this:

Dear Joe [Johanna],
I hope you are quite well. I wrote a letter
before, only I lost it or it got mislaid
Do you play with Elsie and Nora Biddles?
I am learning French, Geometry, Cookery
and Algebra at school now. Dad came
home from France the other week after

*being there ten months, and we all
think the war will be over in a few days.
We are going to get our flags to hang
upstairs in our bedroom. I am sending
two photos, both of me, one of me in a
bathing costume in our backyard.
Uncle Arthur took that, while the other is
me with some fairies up the beck, Elsie
took that one. Rosebud is as fat as ever
and I have made her some new clothes.
How are Teddy and Dolly?*

At first, this seems like an ordinary letter from one girl to another, until you reach the bit about fairies. And even that wouldn't be particularly striking if it weren't for the photographs accompanying the letter, which do actually show Frances with some fairies. The 'beck' to which she refers was a stream at the end of her garden in Cottingley, West Yorkshire, and

Elsie is her cousin, Elsie Wright. This photograph has now become famous the world over. On the back of it was scribbled:

> *Elsie and I are very friendly with the beck Fairies. It is funny that I never used to see them in Africa. It must be too hot for them there.*

The camera they used to take the photograph, belonged to Elsie's father and as he developed the pictures later that day, he was surprised to see some strange white shapes begin to appear: he assumed that they were birds, even though Elsie insisted that they were fairies. Some months later, the girls took another picture with the same camera, this time

of Elsie with a gnome. When her father developed this picture, he assumed the girls must be playing tricks and refused to lend them his camera again. Elsie's parents, Arthur and Polly Wright, tried to find evidence of the girls' trickery, like a cardboard cut-out of a fairy, but to no avail. Some time later, when Polly Wright was at a lecture about 'fairy life' (because she too was interested in the spirit world) given by the Theosophical Society, she mentioned the photographs her daughter had taken. There was immediate interest, and they prints were given to Edward Gardner of the Theosophical society, who had been studying the history of fairies for years and had heard many accounts of fairy sightings.

By an amazing coincidence, Sir Arthur Conan Doyle (the writer who created Sherlock Holmes) had been commissioned by the Strand Magazine to write an article on fairies. He was in the middle of writing his piece when he heard of the two fairy photographs and managed to borrow copies of them. He was suspicious of the photographs at first, as many people were, but photographic experts could not find definitive evidence of the images having been faked. One problem that people had with the pictures was that, the 'fairies' were wearing modern clothes fashionable at the time and had fashionable hairstyles. Also, although the fairies were hovering in the air, there was no evidence of movement in their wings. Sir Arthur Conan Doyle was a firm believer in what he called 'dwellers at the border', or nature

One problem that people had with the pictures was that the 'fairies' were wearing modern clothes fashionable at the time and had fashionable hairstyles.

spirits, but he did not want to be made a fool of, so he had various professionals examine the prints, to see if they were fake or not. Many expressed opinions both ways, but no one could say for sure. Meanwhile, Edward Gardner went to Cottingley with photographic equipment, hoping to persuade Frances and Elsie to take more pictures of fairies at the beck in their back garden, and Sir Arthur Conan Doyle's article on fairies came out in the Strand Magazine, complete with copies of the girls' photographs.

That issue of the magazine sold out within days of publication, and there was a huge public reaction. To many people, these pictures were the long-awaited proof of the existence of a spirit world. But others, often professional scientists, insisted that the photographs were fakes and that the girls should not be encouraged. Perhaps nothing more would have come of it and the story would eventually have faded into history, were it not for the fact that Elsie and Frances did what no one expected them to do and took three more photographs of fairies. Edward Gardner provided the cameras and, in his book *Fairies: a Book of Real Fairies*, published in 1945, he insists that he did not pressurize the girls.

The cameras were loaded, and my final advice was that they need go up to the glen only on fine days as they had been accustomed to do before and 'tice' the fairies, as they called their way of attracting them, and see what they could get. I suggested only the most obvious and easy precautions about lighting and distance, for I knew it was essential they should feel free and unhampered and have no burden of responsibility. If nothing came of it all, I told them, they were not to mind a bit.

Elsie's mother, Polly, wrote to Edward Gardner some months later to say that, 'The morning was dull and misty so they did not take any photos until after dinner when the mist had cleared away and it was sunny I went to my sister's for tea and left them to it. When I got back they had only managed two with fairies, I was disappointed.'

And then again:

They went up again on Saturday afternoon and took several photos but there was only one with anything on and it's a queer one. We can't make it out. Elsie put the plates in this time, and Arthur developed them next day.

P.S. She did not take one flying after all.

One of the photographs showed a fairy offering flowers to Elsie. She said that the flowers were tiny harebells, and that the colors of the fairy's dress were pastel shades of mauve and yellow. Elsie's

father, Arthur, could not bring himself to believe in these fairies. As far as he was concerned, the girls were playing tricks, but her mother supported them since she too believed in the existence of spirits. Reactions to the new fairy photographs were varied. Sir Arthur Conan Doyle was still a strident supporter, but the most common criticism was that the fairies looked suspiciously like the traditional fairies of nursery tales, and that they had very fashionable hairstyles.

The girls went on to take a fifth, and final, photograph of fairies which Conan Doyle describes in detail:

> *Seated on the upper left hand edge with*
> *wings well displayed is an undraped*
> *fairy, apparently considering whether*

it is time to get up. An earlier riser of more mature age is seen on the right possessing abundant hair and wonderful wings. Her slightly denser body can be glimpsed within her fairy dress.

If the Cottingley fairies were genuine, they certainly inhabited the sort of environment we might expect to find them in. The village has both woodland and water and there are oak, ash and thorn trees around the beck.

In deciding for yourselves, whether these were genuine fairy sightings, you might find it helpful to consider the evidence for and against:

Against

• Elsie painted and drew well, and she was obsessed with drawing fairies.

• She was fascinated by the art of photography and had worked at a photographer's studio.

• Both girls had a mischievous sense of humor.

• In a 1971 BBC television interview, Elsie was reluctant to give much detail about the episodes.

• No third party was ever present when the five photographs were taken.

• A professional American illusionist enhanced the pictures and said he could see strings.

• It was also pointed out that some of the fairies resembled those in an illustration in Princess Mary's Gift Book, published in 1914.

For

- Elsie only drew fairies because she saw them so often and, anyway, her drawings are nothing like those in the photographs.

- The illustrations from Princess Mary's Gift Book look something like the fairies they photographed, but only in so far, as most pictures of flying fairies look quite similar.

- The 'string' in the pictures is more likely to be printing streaks.

- The girls simply did not have the material or expertise necessary to fake these photographs.

Later in life, the girls, now old women have hinted that the fairies were cardboard cut-outs, but both still insist that they did see fairies by the beck. Their purpose in producing the photographs was to convince those who refused to believe them. So, even if the Cottingley photographs are fakes, whether or not the girls saw fairies remains an open question.

Fairies in Literature and Legend

In Greek legends, fairies are beautiful maidens in the form of woodland spirits who haunt rivers and streams. They wear a white scarf, which is the mark of their immortality, and if they lose it, they are no longer fairies. Consequently, men who are enchanted by their beauty and want to possess them, make it their goal to take the scarf away from them. Only in this way can they make the fairies human and marry them.

By the time fairies appear in medieval literature, they are already seen as a disappearing race. In many medieval adventure stories, fairies appear to abduct men into their world. They are depicted as frightening but alluring women, who tempt noble knights, trap them and lead them to their ruin.

In Tudor times, fairies were once again figures of fun and frivolity. William Shakespeare has quite a few fairies in his plays, and '*A Midsummer Night's Dream*' is even set partly in the fairy realm, where Oberon and Titania rule as king and queen, although they are constantly at odds with each other. In the play, Oberon decides to play a trick on Titania and he instructs his servant Puck to put a love potion on her eyes which will make her fall in love with the first thing she sees, when she awakens. This happens to be an actor with a

donkey's head on and Titania duly falls head over heals in love with the 'donkey'. However, Puck has made a few mistakes before dousing Titania's eyes with the potion and with some confusing results in the world of humans. In this play, the human world and the fairy world collide, with hilarious results.

When Puck, Oberon's fairy helper, boasts about all the pranks he performs, we get a good insight into the fairy world and the sort of tricks that fairies are renowned for:

I am that merry wanderer of the night.
I jest to Oberon and make him smile
When I a fat and bean-fed horse beguile,
Neighing in likeness of a filly foal:
And sometime lurk I in a gossip's bowl,
In very likeness of a roasted crab,
And when she drinks, against her lips I bob
And on her wither'd dewlap pour the ale.
The wisest aunt, telling the saddest tale,
Sometime for three-foot stool mistaketh me;

Then slip I from her bum, down topples she,
And 'tailor' cries, and falls into a cough;
And then the whole quire hold their hips
and laugh,
And waxen in their mirth and sneeze
and swear
A merrier hour was never wasted there.

Puck's antics are typical of fairy behavior the world over: he is mischievous but without quite being cruel – the worst he does is pretend to be a stool and then slip away just as an old lady sits down on him.

And in another speech he describes, how he loves to confuse people and lead them astray:

I'll follow you, I'll lead you about a round,
Through bog, through bush, through
brake, through brier:
Sometime a horse I'll be, sometime a hound,
A hog, a headless bear, sometime a fire;
And neigh, and bark, and grunt, and roar,
and burn,
Like horse, hound, hog, bear, fire,
at every turn.

This is again, typical of many fairies, illustrating their ability to 'shape-shift', taking on the form of whatever suits their game.

We often think, that all the troublesome things that happen to us, like getting lost and falling off stools, are just bad luck, but really they are the work of fairies having fun at our expense. Knowing

this – that while we are huffing and puffing, fairies somewhere are laughing – can make it a bit better (or worse, perhaps, depending on your mood).

Titania, as the fairy queen, also has a host of young fairies attending on her, with names like Cobweb, Pease-blossom and Moth. One of her fairies tells Puck what she gets up to and in doing so gives us quite a clear impression of a typical fairy's daily life:

I do wander everywhere,
Swifter than the moon's sphere;
And I serve the fairy queen,
To dew her orbs upon the green.
The cowslips tall her pensioners be:
In their gold coats spots you see;
Those be rubies, fairy favours,
In those freckles live their savours:
I must go seek some dewdrops here
And hang a pearl in every cowslip's ear.

This fairy, as you can see, has the job of hanging dewdrops on flowers and grass. You never quite look

at dewdrops in the same way, once you know that they are fairy jewels.

If you ever visit Lego Land in Denmark, you will find on display there Titania's Palace. It is a dollhouse, hand-built by Sir Neville Wilkinson between 1907 and 1922. Titania's Palace has 18 rooms filled with miniature, hand-carved mahogany furniture and there are hundreds of tiny works of art on the walls.

Sir Neville Wilkinson built the palace at the request of his daughter, Gwendolyn, who had seen a fairy running under the roots of a tree in a wood, near the family home in Ireland. Gwendolyn felt sorry for the fairies, who were forced to live underground in the cold and dark, and so her father made the palace as a home for them.

Peter Pan

In J. M. Barrie's Peter Pan stories, there is a fairy called Tinker Bell. She guides Peter Pan through the world of Never Never Land, sprinkling fairy dust as she flies. Tinker Bell has a voice like a tinkling bell and she got the name 'Tinker' because she mends the pots and pans, which is what a tin worker, or 'tinker' does. In Peter Pan, we are given a different version of the origin of fairies, one more poetical and perhaps more fanciful:

"When the first baby laughed for the first time, the laugh broke into a thousand pieces and they all went skipping about, and that was the beginning of fairies."

So, according to this story, a fairy is actually a piece of the first baby's laugh! It is also said in Peter Pan that every time a child says they don't believe in fairies, somewhere a fairy falls down dead. And, in the story, Tinker Bell will die if children stop believing in fairies. Tinker Bell is a bold fairy, who says what she thinks and is not afraid of anyone. She is fiercely loyal to Peter Pan and inclined to be jealous of any other females who hang around him. This can lead her to act in a spiteful way, and she has been known to scratch, pinch and pull hair in fits of jealous rage. Tinker Bell is a classic example of the fairy character – well-intentioned and loving, but certainly, not perfect. Her possessiveness is her great weakness, but generally she is faithful, trustworthy and cheerful.

"When the first baby laughed for the first time, the laugh broke into a thousand pieces and they all went skipping about, and that was the beginning of fairies."

Pinocchio

In Carlo Collodi's story Pinocchio, a wooden puppet is made into a real boy when he receives the gift of life from the Blue Fairy. The Blue Fairy shows the puppet Pinocchio boundless love and kindness and, although she is always advising him not to do bad things, she always forgives his errors and gives him another chance. She is always telling him "First the medicine and then the sugar," but he never listens and always wants the sugar first, but then won't take the medicine. Eventually, Pinocchio realizes what constant loving kindness he has been shown by the Blue Fairy, even though he has behaved badly, and he resolves to be better just for her. As a reward, the Blue Fairy finally grants him the one wish he has always held dear. That, of becoming a real, live boy.

The Blue Fairy is far more mature and wise than Tinker Bell, and always has a child's best interests at heart. She is more of a sensible, kind mother figure than a cheeky imp like Tinker Bell. In fact, she is really not just a fairy, but a fairy godmother. It is said that we all have a fairy godmother, who watches over us and tells us in a quiet voice which seems to come from inside us how we should and shouldn't behave.

Sugar Plum Fairy

Another famous fairy is the Sugar Plum Fairy who appears in Tchaikovsky's ballet 'The Nutcracker'. Sugar Plum Fairies in general are quite shy. They live in orchards and generally only come out at blossom time in spring and in late summer when the ripe, sweet

The Secret History Of Fairies

fruit is falling to the ground. They love the dawn chorus when birds sing their hearts out and it is at this time that you would most likely see one, perhaps resting sleepily in the branches of a plum tree listening to the music. In The Nutcracker, the Sugar Plum Fairy, with all her busy attendants, welcomes Clara to her court in the Kingdom of Sweets. The famous music of the Nutcracker Suite strikes up and coffee, tea,

But the fairy we will all be most familiar with is the Tooth Fairy. She is perhaps the last surviving fairy who is still allowed an existence in our culture. The Tooth Fairy is part of a great tradition of Household Brownies who perform useful tasks in the home

chocolate and sugar candy dance with clowns and toy flutes, accompanying the Sugar Plum Fairy and her prince around the floor. At the end of the ball, the Sugar Plum Fairy grants Clara her wish, which is to dance with the Prince.

But the fairy we will all be most familiar with is the Tooth Fairy. She is perhaps, the last surviving fairy who is still allowed an existence in our culture. The Tooth Fairy is part of a great tradition of Household Brownies who perform useful tasks in the home, often

taking things we have no use for (like teeth which have fallen out) and exchanging them with treasure of some value. It is not known what fairies do with the teeth they collect, but they are certain to have some use for them. It is easy to imagine them as stools or tables furnishing a fairy home.

There are instances in literature of human and fairy inter-marriage, but it does not always go well.

There is a general idea that fairies were around once, but not any longer. This is simply not the case.

It is true that pollution, expansion of cities and technological advances are all responsible for the decline in the fairy population, but they are still there. It's just that we are no longer prepared to look and listen closely enough, and we are all too busy to stop and be still long enough to appreciate the fairies all around us.